"Gorgeous Reflections: Empowering Selfie Coloring Book for Black Women Adults"

€ 2023 by Selena L.L. Arnold All rights reserved.

Unauthorized use or reproduction of any portion of this book is strictly prohibited without the author's prior written consent, except for brief quotations allowed for book reviews.

Hello Beautiful

This Journal Belongs To:

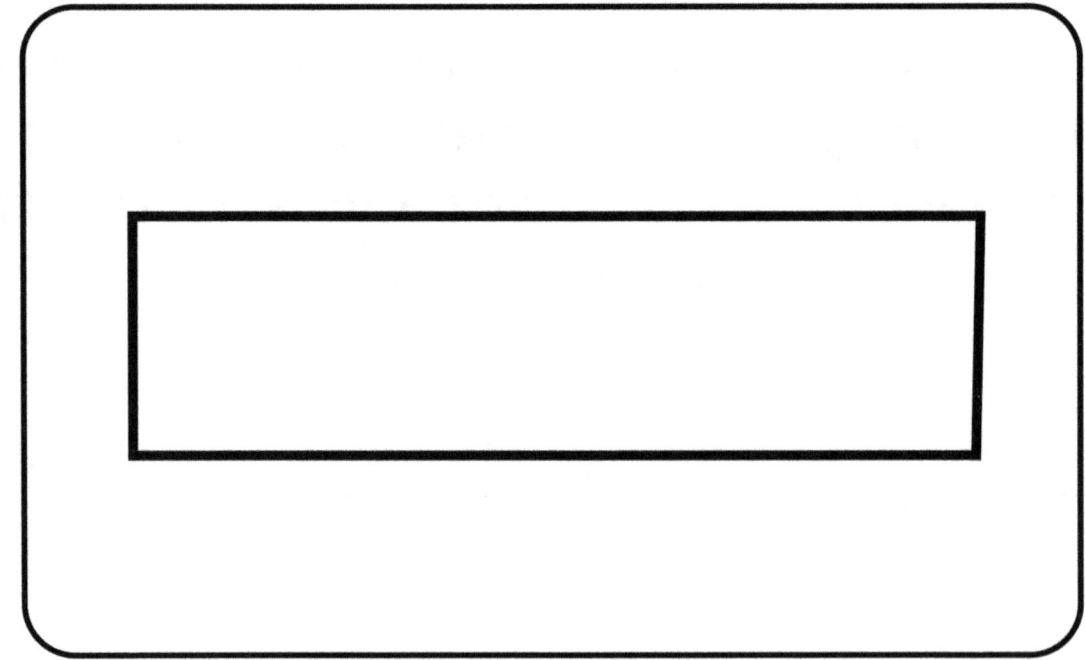

Embrace your unique beauty; let it shine brightly.

Radiate confidence with every stroke of color.

Celebrate your essence; you are a masterpiece.

Bold hues mirror your vibrant spirit and strength.

Each shade tells a story; your story is beautiful.

Embody the colors of resilience and grace.

Beauty is diversity; find it within your palette.

Reflect the hues of your soul; you are extraordinary.

In every color, find a piece of your magnificent journey.

Your colors are your voice; speak boldly, radiate love.

Be the artist of your own identity; paint it vividly.

With each color, embrace your heritage and ancestry.

Embrace the spectrum of your emotions; you are whole.

Your beauty knows no bounds; let the colors show it.

Evoke the power of self-love in every shade you choose.

Find peace in the tranquility of your chosen colors.

Unleash your creativity; paint your world

"Every color is a chapter in your story; make it a masterpiece."

"May your colors inspire others to paint their own beautiful lives."

"May your colors inspire others to paint their own beautiful lives."

"Embrace the mosaic of your emotions; each color tells a tale."

"Your creativity is boundless; let it soar with every color."

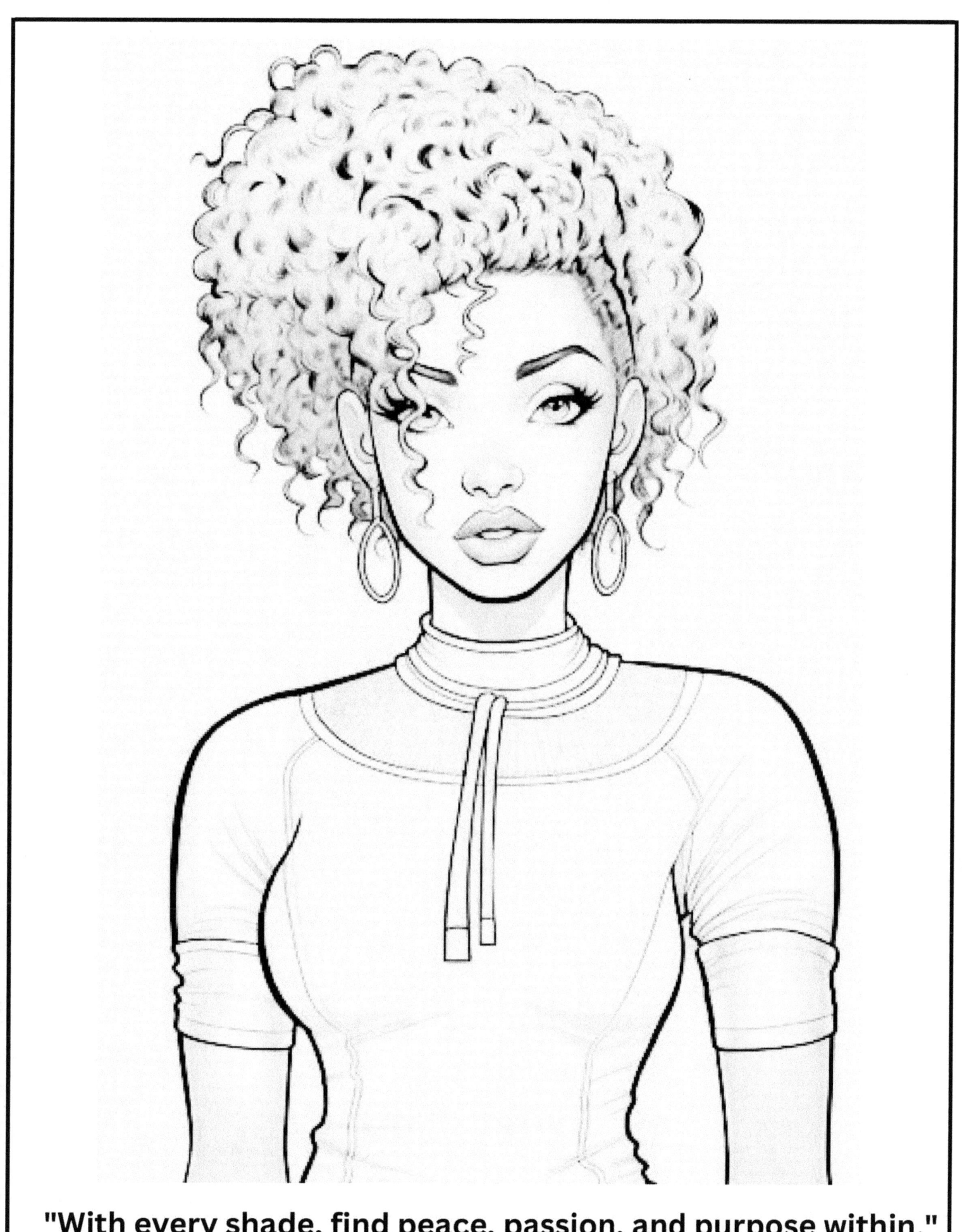

"With every shade, find peace, passion, and purpose within."

"Celebrate diversity; every color adds to your brilliance."

"Your colors reflect the depth of your spirit; shine brightly."

"Paint your dreams with the vibrant hues of your aspirations."

"Colors whisper the language of your heart; listen and embrace."

"In every stroke, celebrate the essence of who you are."

"In the world of colors, you are the artist of your destiny."

"May your colors reflect the joy within; share it with the world."

"Color outside the lines; your uniqueness is your strength."

"Your creativity knows no boundaries; express it boldly."

"With every stroke, weave the tapestry of your wonderful existence."

"Let your imagination dance freely in the colors of your choice."

"In every color, find a reason to smile, to hope, to dream."

www.ingramcontent.com/pod-product-compliance
Lightning Source LLC
LaVergne TN
LVHW081614060526
838201LV00054B/2241